W9-ACP-485

A FIRST LOOK AT
AMERICA'S
PRESIDENTS

JOHN QUINCY ADAMS

The 6th President

by Diane Bailey

Consultant: Philip Nash
Associate Professor of History
Pennsylvania State University
Sharon, Pennsylvania

BEARPORT
PUBLISHING

New York, New York

Credits

Cover, Courtesy White House Historical Association; 4, © Joseph Sohm/Shutterstock; 5, Courtesy White House; 7T, Courtesy Howard Pyle/Delaware Museum of Art/Wiki; 7B, Courtesy Navy History and Heritage Command; 8, © Chee-on Long/DT; 9T, Courtesy National Portrait Gallery; 9R, Courtesy Massachusetts Fine Art Gallery; 9B, Courtesy Web Gallery of Art; 10, © Art Resource; 12, Courtesy Geographica Rare Antique Maps/Wikimedia; 13T, Courtesy Metropolitan Museum of Art; 13B, Courtesy National Archives; 14, Courtesy National Portrait Gallery; 15T, Courtesy Indiana Historical Society; 15B, Courtesy historical-markers.org; 16, Courtesy Lawrence Jackson/White House; 17T, © Everett Historical/Shutterstock; 17B, © Michael Kodas/MCT/Newscom; 18, Courtesy House of Representatives; 19, Courtesy National Archives; 20T, Courtesy Navy History and Heritage Command; 20B, Courtesy Howard Pyle/Delaware Museum of Art; 21TL, Courtesy National Portrait Gallery; 21TR, © Splosh/Dreamstime; 21B, Courtesy Lawrence Jackson/White House; 22, Courtesy John Lopez Studios.

Publisher: Kenn Goin
Senior Editor: Joyce Tavolacci
Creative Director: Spencer Brinker
Production and Photo Research: Shoreline Publishing Group LLC

Library of Congress Cataloging-in-Publication Data

Names: Bailey, Diane, 1966– author. | Nash, Philip, consultant.
Title: John Quincy Adams : the 6th president / by Diane Bailey ; Consultant:
   Philip Nash, Associate Professor of History, Pennsylvania State University.
Description: New York, New York : Bearport Publishing Company, Inc., 2017. |
   Series: A first look at America's presidents | Includes bibliographical
   references and index. | Audience: Ages 4–6._
Identifiers: LCCN 2016012116 (print) | LCCN 2016012626 (ebook) | ISBN
   9781944102654 (library binding) | ISBN 9781944997359 (ebook)
Subjects: LCSH: Adams, John Quincy, 1767-1848—Juvenile literature. |
   Presidents—United States—Biography—Juvenile literature.
Classification: LCC E377 .B316 2017 (print) | LCC E377 (ebook) | DDC
   973.5/5092—dc23
LC record available at http://lccn.loc.gov/2016012116

For more information, write to Bearport Publishing Company, Inc., 45 West 21st Street, Suite 3B, New York, New York 10010. Printed in the United States of America.

10 9 8 7 6 5 4 3 2 1

CONTENTS

Working for America

John Quincy Adams worked hard for America. He was a **diplomat**, a congressman, and the president. In every job he held, Adams was independent and strong. He helped make the United States strong, too.

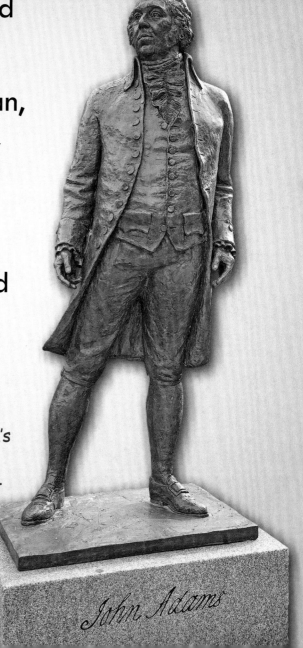

John Quincy's father, John Adams, was America's second president. He served from 1797 to 1801.

John Quincy Adams was the sixth president. He served from 1825 to 1829.

Going to Europe

John Quincy Adams was born in 1767 in the **colony** of Massachusetts. As a boy, he went to France with his father. John was very bright and curious. At age 14, he got a job working for the U.S. **ambassador** to Russia!

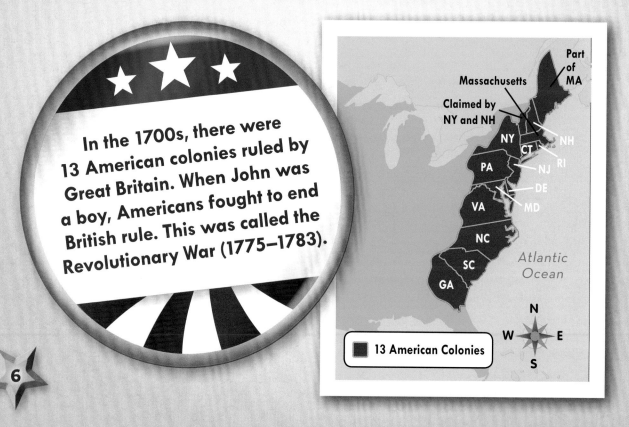

In the 1700s, there were 13 American colonies ruled by Great Britain. When John was a boy, Americans fought to end British rule. This was called the Revolutionary War (1775–1783).

Part of MA

Massachusetts

Claimed by NY and NH

NY
CT
NH
RI
PA
NJ
DE
VA
MD
NC
SC
GA

Atlantic Ocean

N
W E
S

■ 13 American Colonies

In 1775, John saw a Revolutionary War battle from his home. It was the Battle of Bunker Hill.

John and his father sailed to France on a ship. Along the way, the ship ran into trouble. John helped bail water out of it to save it from sinking!

Speaking Up

When Adams grew up, he became a lawyer. He was outspoken and stood up for his beliefs. President George Washington liked these qualities. In 1794, Washington gave Adams a job as a diplomat.

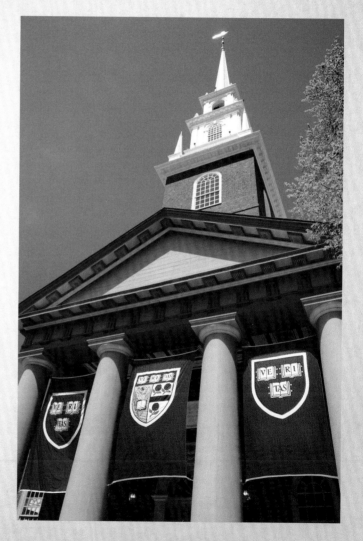

Adams went to Harvard College in Massachusetts.

Adams as
a young adult

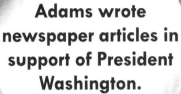

Adams wrote
newspaper articles in
support of President
Washington.

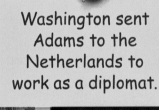

Washington sent
Adams to the
Netherlands to
work as a diplomat.

9

Ending a War

Adams was good at talking to people and solving problems. In 1812, Great Britain and the United States went to war. To bring peace, Adams worked with other diplomats. Together, they wrote a peace **treaty** that ended the war.

This painting shows the signing of the peace treaty in 1814.

Adams

The peace agreement was called the Treaty of Ghent. Ghent is the city in Belgium where the treaty was signed.

11

Making a Strong Country

In 1817, Adams became **secretary of state**. He worked with President James Monroe to make America bigger and stronger. Together, they created an important new policy. It was called the Monroe Doctrine. It warned Europe to stay out of America's affairs.

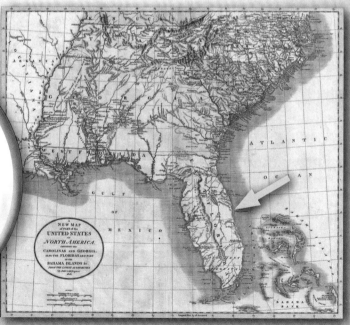

Florida once belonged to Spain. Adams helped make Florida part of the United States.

James Monroe was president from 1817 to 1825.

Adams's passport when he was secretary of state, which allowed him to travel to other countries

13

Big Ideas

In 1824, Adams ran for president. It was a close race, but Adams won. As president, he worked to improve transportation. In the early 1800s, traveling was slow and difficult. Adams started projects to build better roads and **canals**. They helped connect people all over America!

John Quincy Adams as president

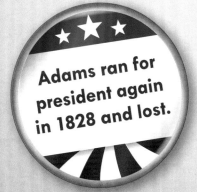

Adams ran for president again in 1828 and lost.

The Erie Canal was completed while Adams was president. The canal made it easier to transport goods and people.

Adams helped to extend the National Road. When it was finished, it stretched from Maryland to Illinois.

THE NATIONAL ROAD
(CALLED THE CUMBERLAND ROAD)

WAS THE FIRST OF THE INTERNAL IMPROVEMENTS UNDERTAKEN BY THE U. S. GOVERNMENT. SURVEYS WERE AUTHORIZED IN 1806 OVER THE ROUTE OF "BRADDOCK'S ROAD", WHICH FOLLOWED "NEMACOLIN'S PATH", AN INDIAN TRAIL, OVER WHICH GEORGE WASHINGTON TRAVELED IN 1754 TO FORT LeBOEUF.

STATE ROADS COMMISSION

15

Fighting for Freedom

After leaving office, Adams missed being in government. In 1830, he was elected to the House of Representatives, a part of Congress. He was a powerful leader who fought for people's rights. At the time, slavery was allowed in many states. Adams worked hard to end slavery.

Adams is the only person to serve in the House of Representatives after being president.

In 1839, a group of Africans took over a ship where they were being held as slaves. The Africans were captured and arrested. In a famous court case, Adams fought for their freedom.

Joseph Cinqué, one of the African leaders who was arrested

The slave ship was called *La Amistad.*

A Last Speech

On February 21, 1848, Adams collapsed while giving a speech. He died two days later. Today, we remember his loyalty to America. He fought for peace. He helped make the country strong and free.

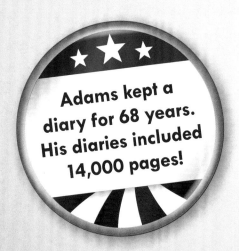

Adams kept a diary for 68 years. His diaries included 14,000 pages!

Adams died in this room in the Capitol Building in Washington, DC. The room is still used by members of Congress.

Adams was one of the first presidents to have his photo taken.

19

TIMELINE

Here are some major events from John Quincy Adams's life.

1767
Adams is born in Massachusetts.

1778
Adams goes to Europe for the first time.

1794
Adams becomes a diplomat.

1760   1770   1780   1790   1800

1775–1783
The Revolutionary War

1787
Adams graduates from Harvard College.

1817
Adams becomes secretary of state.

1825
Adams is elected president.

1848
Adams dies in the Capitol Building.

1810	1820	1830	1840	1850

1831
Adams joins the U.S. House of Representatives.

1841
Adams helps win the *La Amistad* case.

"If your actions inspire others to dream more, learn more, do more, and become more, you are a leader."

"Always vote for principle, though you may vote alone."

Adams liked to write poetry. One poem was 2,000 lines long!

Adams had a pet alligator that lived in a bathtub in the White House!

"Try and fail, but don't fail to try."

GLOSSARY

ambassador (am-BASS-uh-dur) the top person who represents his or her country in another country

canals (kuh-NALZ) manmade waterways

colony (KOL-uh-nee) an area that has been settled by people from another country and is ruled by that country

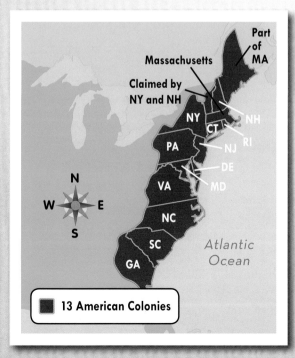

diplomat (DIP-luh-mat) a person who represents his or her country in another country

secretary of state (SEK-ruh-tair-ee UHV STAYT) the U.S official who deals with other countries

treaty (TREE-tee) an agreement between two or more countries

23

Index

Read More

Barnes, Peter W. *President Adams' Alligator: And Other White House Pets.* Washington, DC: Little Patriot Press (2013).

Hopkinson, Deborah. *John Adams Speaks for Freedom (Stories of Famous Americans).* New York: Simon Spotlight (2005).

Souter, Gerry, and Janet Souter. *John Quincy Adams: Our Sixth President (Presidents of the U.S.A.).* Mankato, MN: The Child's World (2004).

Learn More Online

To learn more about John Quincy Adams, visit
www.bearportpublishing.com/AmericasPresidents

About the Author:
Diane Bailey has
written dozens
of books for kids.
She lives in Kansas.